Masters of Music

THE WORLD'S GREATEST COMPOSERS

The Life and Times of

Johannes Brahms

Mitchell Lane
PUBLISHERS

P.O. Box 196
Hockessin, Delaware 19707

Masters of Music

THE WORLD'S GREATEST COMPOSERS

Titles in the Series

The Life and Times of...

Visit us on the web: www.mitchelllane.com
Comments? email us: mitchelllane@mitchelllane.com

Masters of Music
THE WORLD'S GREATEST COMPOSERS

The Life and Times of
Johannes Brahms

by Jim Whiting

Printing   1   2   3   4   5   6   7   8
        Library of Congress Cataloging-in-Publication Data
Whiting, Jim, 1943-
        The life and times of Johannes Brahms/Jim Whiting.
               p. cm. — (Masters of music. The world's greatest composers)
        Summary: A biography of the nineteenth-century German composer of many works for
        individual instruments, voices, orchestras, and choirs, including "Wiegenlied" or "Cradle
        Song," popularly known as "Brahms Lullaby."
        Includes bibliographical references (p.) and index.
               ISBN 1-58415-214-1 (lib bdg.)
        1. Brahms, Johannes, 1833-1897—Juvenile literature. 2. Composers—Germany—Biogra-
        phy—Juvenile literature. [1. Brahms, Johannes, 1833-1897. 2. Composers.] I. Title. II.
        Series.
        ML3930.B75W45 2003
        780'.92—dc21   2003000350

ABOUT THE AUTHOR: Jim Whiting has been a journalist, writer, editor, and photographer for more than 20 years. In addition to a lengthy stint as publisher of *Northwest Runner* magazine, Mr. Whiting has contributed articles to the *Seattle Times*, *Conde Nast Traveler*, *Newsday*, and *Saturday Evening Post*. He has edited more than 20 titles in the Mitchell Lane Real-Life Reader Biography series and Unlocking the Secrets of Science. His love of classical music inspired him to write this book. He lives in Washington state with his wife and two teenage sons.

PUBLISHER'S NOTE: This story is based on the author's extensive research, which he believes to be accurate. Documentation of such research is contained on page 46.

The internet sites referenced herein were active as of the publication date. Due to the fleeting nature of some Web sites, we cannot guarantee they will all be active when you are reading this book.

Contents

The Life and Times of
Johannes Brahms

by Jim Whiting

* For Your Information

Johannes Brahms as he appeared at about the age of 30. Compare this illustration with the one on p. 36, taken just a few years later. By then, Brahms had grown his famous beard.

CHAPTER I

High Expectations

A long article in a popular German music magazine declared him a "Young eagle!" and a "Genius!"

The year was 1853, and twenty-year-old Johannes Brahms must have been thrilled. He had grown up in poverty and hardly anyone had heard of him. Yet Robert Schumann, a famous composer he had known for barely two weeks, had just written this glowing recommendation about him. According to Schumann, young Brahms "would be chosen to express the most exalted spirit of the times in an ideal manner." His life in virtual obscurity would be over.

The exposure from the article was both a blessing and a curse. It did bring almost overnight fame to Brahms, but it also aroused jealousy among other musicians and put extraordinary expectations on his compositions. Now that he had been proclaimed as a genius, anything less than the highest quality could be considered a failure. And while Schumann's praise may have opened the door for financial success, Brahms still had to work hard to make a living.

It would have been understandable if he had crumpled under all this pressure. He didn't.

In fact, he became so successful that the history of classical music for many people is contained in a single phrase: The Three B's. The phrase refers to three composers:

Johann Sebastian Bach

Ludwig van Beethoven

Johannes Brahms

Their lives span just over two centuries, from Bach's birth in 1685 to Brahms's death in 1897.

Of the three, Brahms enjoyed the greatest financial rewards and recognition during his lifetime. Part of the reason for this success was that Brahms was born at the right time. Earlier composers such as Bach, Beethoven, and Wolfgang Mozart were usually dependent on the support of wealthy aristocrats or religious groups. But by Brahms's time, classical music was at the peak of its popularity among the general population. It was finally possible for a composer to earn a good living on his own.

Because of the demands that had been placed on him at a young age, Brahms was always conscious of what was expected of him. Late in his life he went back through his early compositions. Many had never been published. These would have been valuable to music historians in tracing his development. Because they didn't meet his high personal standards, he destroyed them.

Another result of this early praise was that Brahms did not write his first symphony until 1876, when he was forty-three. At a corresponding age Beethoven had written eight. Franz Schubert, who lived at about the same time as Beethoven, had composed nine by the time of his untimely death at the age of thirty-two.

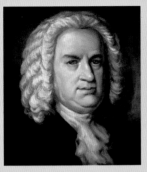

Johann Sebastian Bach, Ludwig van Beethoven and Johannes Brahms (from left to right) are sometimes known as classical music's "Three B's" because their last names all begin with the letter B. Many people consider them as the three greatest composers who ever lived.

And Mozart wrote forty-one before his death at the age of thirty-five.

Because he lived in Vienna, Austria, Brahms was all too conscious of his position as Beethoven's successor. Beethoven had also lived there, and even though he had died six years before Brahms was born, the great man's legacy hovered over him. Brahms didn't want to try writing a symphony until he felt completely confident in his ability.

"Composing a symphony is no laughing matter," he repeatedly said to those who urged him to compose one. "You have no idea of how it feels to hear behind you the tramp of a giant like Beethoven."

As soon as the symphony appeared, it was compared to works by Beethoven. Hans von Bülow, a famous conductor, referred to it as The Tenth, as if it were yet another symphony by Beethoven. In tribute, Brahms included a hint of the famous "Ode to Joy" theme from Beethoven's Ninth Symphony in the final movement of his first symphony.

These weren't the only similarities between the two men. Both grew up in German cities several hundred miles from Vienna. Both were sloppy in their personal habits. Both had short tempers. Neither was ever married. They even walked in much the same way, leaning forward slightly with their hands behind their backs. ◆

Hans von Bülow was a famous German classical music conductor. He was born in 1830 and died in 1894. He was also an excellent pianist and composer.

PHOTOGRAPHY FYInfo

One of the differences between Brahms and earlier composers such as Beethoven and Mozart is that we have photographs of Brahms. We have to rely on paintings and drawings to form an idea of the appearance of his predecessors.

George Eastman and Thomas Edison

The key year was 1839, when the photographic process was made available to the public. About that time Sir John Herschel coined the word *photography* (which literally means "writing with light"). From that point on, almost anyone who was famous began having his or her picture taken. So did a lot of people who weren't famous.

The first actual photograph was produced in 1826 by a Frenchman named Joseph Nicéphore Niepce. He used a small camera obscura with a metal plate treated with chemicals to make an image of the landscape outside his window. The exposure lasted eight hours. Niepce called the process a heliograph ("writing with the sun"). In 1829 he became partners with Louis Daguerre, who advanced the process and made it possible to produce pictures called daguerreotypes.

Not everyone liked the idea. Many portrait painters saw photography as a threat to their livelihood. They created a pun on the word *foe,* which means "enemy," and called it a "foe-to-graphic art." But their opposition didn't slow down the improvements that kept coming.

But cameras still had one drawback. They were large, cumbersome, and needed special training to operate them.

That changed in 1888. American inventor George Eastman developed a small box camera. He founded the Eastman Kodak Company in 1892 and introduced the slogan, "You press the button, we do the rest." Now anyone could take photographs. For a long time the word *Kodak* was almost synonymous with *camera.*

Many advances followed. Shutter speeds faster than 1/4000 second allowed photographers to freeze motion. Multiple exposures created strange effects. Color film let us see the world as it really is.

And much more recently, the invention of digital photography eliminated film altogether. Now photographers—both professionals and parents taking pictures of their children—can see their results almost instantly.

The birthplace of Johannes Brahms in a tenement in the city of Hamburg, Germany. Many families were crowded into this building. The Brahms family only had two rooms to themselves.

Masters of Music

CHAPTER 2

Playing the Piano in Poverty

Johannes Brahms was born on May 7, 1833, to Johann Jakob and Christiane Brahms. He was the couple's second child. He joined Elisabeth, who was born in 1831. Another son, Fritz, would be born two years after Johannes.

Johann Jakob was descended from craftspeople and tradesmen. His father, an innkeeper, was horrified when his growing son showed musical inclinations. He promptly forbade the boy to have anything more to do with music. But as happens with many teenagers, Johann Jakob defied his father. He even cut school to learn how to play music. There were many arguments, and the boy ran away from home several times. Finally his father gave in. Young Johann Jakob could take music lessons.

When Johann Jakob was nineteen he moved to Hamburg, one of Germany's largest cities. The job market there was tough. Even though he played several instruments, the only work he could find was in places such as taverns and dance halls. He didn't make much money and lived in a series of small dirty apartments.

Then he moved into a vacant room in a house that Christiane shared with her sister and brother-in-law. A week later he proposed

This sketch of Johannes Brahms was made when he was 20. The artist is J.B. Laurens, and the original hangs in the Carpentras Museum in southern France.

marriage. He was twenty-four at the time, and his would-be bride was forty-one. At first she thought he was joking. He was strong and handsome, while she was somewhat frail and not very attractive. But he was completely sincere. Though she had some misgivings about the age difference, her brother-in-law urged her to accept. It would be her last chance for a home and children, he said. She agreed to become Johann Jakob's wife. The marriage began in 1830 and prospered for many years.

Christiane Brahms was no stranger to hard work. At the age of thirteen she began working as a seamstress. She would often come home after a full day of sewing and help with chores until midnight. Later she worked as a household servant, a job she held for ten years. Eventually she opened a sewing shop with her sister. Then Johann Jakob came along.

Although he tried hard, Johann Jakob's earnings were meager. The family lived in poverty. They had to move several times. Johannes was born in a crowded six-story apartment house that faced a narrow alley. The Brahmses occupied two small rooms, a combination kitchen and entrance plus a larger living room with a closet where the family slept. In spite of their poverty, both parents, especially Christiane, did their best to make wherever they lived a loving, peaceful and secure home.

Johannes, whose family nicknamed him Hannes, grew up like many other youngsters. From an early age he enjoyed playing with miniature lead soldiers—something that he continued well into his adult life.

He began attending a private school at the age of six, then transferred to another one at the age of eleven. He studied Latin, French, English, mathematics, and natural history.

But his natural gifts and interests lay in music. His father, still with vivid memories of the rebellion that made his own music career possible, approved. Hannes began taking lessons at the age of four from Johann Jakob. Johann Jakob may have envisioned his son rising to become a member of the Hamburg Philharmonic, the city's largest and most prestigious orchestra. For a man who scraped out a bare living playing in cafés, theaters, and waterfront taverns, that must have seemed the height of ambition.

The youngster appears to have inherited more than a love of music from his father. He quickly proved that he was his father's son as a rebel. Johann Jakob wanted Hannes to learn how to play the stringed instruments with which he was familiar. But Hannes wanted to be a pianist. His father was horrified. The Hamburg Philharmonic didn't even have a pianist. When Hannes was seven, Johann Jakob finally gave in. Hannes began taking piano lessons from Friedrich Cossel, a noted Hamburg teacher.

Cossel recognized that his young pupil had a great deal of natural ability. Though he wasn't much better off financially than the Brahms family, he devoted much of his time to Hannes. It wasn't unusual for the boy to spend the entire day with his teacher, and soon Cossel moved closer to the Brahmses.

Three years later Hannes was good enough to perform in public. Not even a wagon that ran over his chest and put him in bed for six weeks could deter him. His father arranged a chamber music concert to showcase his son's abilities. The money that was raised would help finance his further studies.

The event also resulted in what promised to be a life-changing offer. A concert promoter was in the audience. He pulled Johann Jakob aside and said he would sponsor Hannes on a tour of the United States. He would be presented as a child prodigy, much like

Wolfgang Mozart had been nearly a century before him. The rest of the family could accompany him.

Not surprisingly, the parents were excited. This could be their ticket out of poverty.

Christiane was especially enthusiastic. "We can live in hotels and I won't have to do any more scrubbing," she told a friend. After more than thirty years of toil and drudgery, the chance to enjoy a better life was very appealing.

There was one serious objection: Cossel feared this career path would destroy the boy's talent. Hannes was a gifted musician, Cossel felt, but not a true child prodigy. Even if he were, most prodigies quickly burned out and were soon forgotten. He had better things in mind for his prize pupil.

Cossel made a genuine sacrifice. He decided to give up teaching the boy to whom he had devoted so much time, energy, and caring. He wanted to turn him over to Eduard Marxsen, who was perhaps Hamburg's most famous teacher. He hoped that Marxsen's reputation would help persuade the parents not to accept the promoter's offer.

Cossel's plan ran into a hitch. Marxsen wasn't interested in teaching Brahms. He heard Hannes play and didn't feel that the boy had the ability or the interest to become a true piano virtuoso.

Cossel persisted, and finally Marxsen relented. He would teach the youngster.

At some point the combined efforts of Cossel and Marxsen prevailed on Johann Jakob and Christiane. The Brahmses would remain in Hamburg. There would be no trip to the United States.

Marxsen built on the strong foundation that Cossel had laid, then added a new aspect. Though Cossel had objected to Hannes's efforts at composing, Marxsen encouraged the boy to continue writing music. He also gave him formal training in music theory and composition. Marxsen's input was extremely valuable. He had studied with several men who had been personally acquainted with the great classical composers Beethoven, Franz Schubert, Franz Joseph Haydn, and Mozart. These composers formed the most enduring influences on the way that Brahms would later write his own music.

It didn't take long for Marxsen to form a new opinion of his pupil. Composition, not piano playing, was Hannes's greatest strength.

When he began his lessons with Marxsen, Johannes Brahms was set firmly in his life's direction, a direction that would eventually make him famous far beyond the wildest dreams of his poverty-filled youth. ◆

The Nobel Prizes

Every fall the world waits to learn who will be awarded the Nobel Prizes. These awards are given to the individuals who do the most to advance human understanding in six different areas: peace, literature, physics, chemistry, economics, and medicine or physiology. The awards are named for Alfred Nobel, the man who created them and provided the original funding.

Nobel was born on October 21, 1833—just a few months after Brahms—in Stockholm, Sweden. At his father's insistence, Alfred studied chemical engineering. While in Paris, France, he met an Italian chemist named Ascanio Sobrero, who had invented an explosive compound called nitroglycerin. It was a liquid that was considered dangerously unstable and therefore without any practical value. Alfred began working to find a way of making nitroglycerin safe to handle. That way it could be used in construction work.

He had a few accidents. One of them, in 1864, resulted in the death of several people, including Alfred's beloved younger brother. Alfred was ordered to move outside the Stockholm city limits. He set up a new laboratory on a barge on a nearby lake.

Eventually Alfred discovered that he could mix nitroglycerin with silica, a substance similar to sand. That converted the liquid into a paste, which could then be put into tubes that were much less risky to handle. He called his invention dynamite and patented it in 1867. Then he invented blasting caps, which would ignite the dynamite when lit by a fuse. This combination made it much cheaper and less dangerous to do the blasting work necessary for building tunnels and roads. As a result, Alfred Nobel soon became a very rich man.

Alfred was concerned about the destructive potential of his invention. He wanted to counterbalance that potential with something constructive—to reward human ingenuity that was used for "the greatest benefit [to] mankind." When he died on December 10, 1896, his will directed that most of his estate go to establish the prizes that bear his name. Since he had many other inventions that had also been profitable—such as artificial rubber and silk—his estate contained a great deal of money.

The Nobel Prizes are presented every year on December 10, the anniversary of Alfred Nobel's death. The prestige of being a Nobel Prize winner is considered priceless.

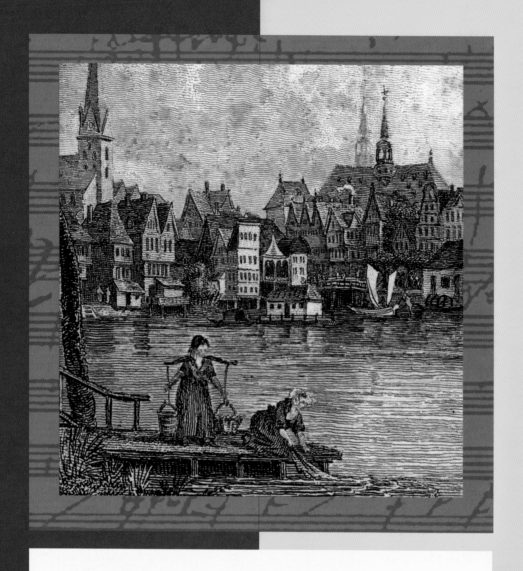

Johannes Brahms was born in the city of Hamburg. It is a major seaport that is located about 25 miles upstream from the mouth of the Elbe River in northern Germany.

The First Strides Toward Success

When Brahms was barely thirteen, there still wasn't much money coming into the house. His mother had already been helping out her family at that age. Hannes had to do the same.

He began a series of jobs similar to those that his father had held. Hamburg was a major seaport. Its skyline was etched with the tall masts of sailing ships that were tied up at the docks. Every day hundreds of sailors would come ashore looking for entertainment. There were dozens of taverns near the docks, and one of the cheapest forms of entertainment was listening to music and dancing. Hannes had no trouble finding employment playing in these places. It was not uncommon for him to receive calls to play for wild parties that sometimes lasted until dawn.

The demanding schedule was hard on the youngster. During the day he took lessons and played some of the finest music that has ever been written. At night he spent endless hours in places that could not have been very uplifting. The language he heard would have been coarse. The air was probably filled with smoke from pipes and cigarettes. He would have been surrounded by drunken people. He was a thin, frail boy to begin with. Living as he did, he became even weaker and sometimes almost ill. Once he wrote that he "could only walk along an avenue by staggering from tree to tree, otherwise I would have fallen."

Then he got lucky. A friend of his father's invited him to stay in a country village during the summers of 1847 and 1848 and give piano lessons to his daughter. While there, Hannes also conducted the village choir. These duties left him with plenty of time for composing. The change of scenery, fresh air, and good food, plus long walks and swimming in the nearby river, did wonders for the sickly boy. He returned after the second summer as a robust young man and enjoyed excellent health for the rest of his life.

Soon after returning from his second idyllic summer, he gave his first solo piano recital, with a second one the following spring. But he was only sixteen—there were many excellent and more experienced pianists in the city. International stars also played there.

By then he realized that his destiny lay in composition.

Certainly Marxsen thought so. Not long after the famous composer Felix Mendelssohn died in late 1847, Marxsen told friends, "A great master of the musical art has gone hence, but an even greater one will bloom for us in Brahms."

Brahms's single-minded devotion to his music meant that he had little free time to spend with other people his own age. The shy young man had virtually no friends. He wasn't even that friendly with his own brother. Hannes and Fritz were both musicians. As the older brother and the better musician, Hannes received the best of everything. Fritz got what was left over. Because the Brahms family was so poor, that was very little indeed. Not surprisingly, Fritz was resentful. This resentment increased even more in later life when he was referred to as "the wrong Brahms."

A picture of Johannes Brahms (standing) with the famous Hungarian violinist Eduard Reményi. Brahms' first musical tour began at the age of 20 when he accompanied Reményi.

When Johannes was twenty-six, his mother wrote, "Oh, what Fritz could have learned from you, had you behaved like real brothers!"

His father too may have felt an increasing sense of frustration. His elder son had received the finest in musical instruction. At nearly twenty years old, he had very little to show for all those years of training. Johannes had a reputation as a competent piano player, but there was very little else.

Again the young man would have a stroke of luck.

This time it came in the form of a virtuoso violinist named Eduard Reményi. Reményi had had to leave his native Hungary in 1848 because of his political activities. He settled in Hamburg. Eventually he met Brahms and in 1853 invited him to come along on a concert tour.

When they arrived at the court of Hanover, the pair met Johann Joachim, another famous violinist. Joachim, who was only two years older than Brahms, already had an international reputation. Brahms overcame his shyness, and the two men became fast friends. They often talked long into the night.

When it was time to depart, Joachim gave Brahms a glowing letter of introduction to the famous composer Franz Liszt. Joachim knew that Liszt liked to support up-and-coming musicians. But the meeting didn't go well. Liszt insisted that the classically trained Brahms compose what was known as "new German" music. Brahms, again showing his stubbornness, refused. On top of that, he made it clear that he didn't think much of Liszt's own work.

Reményi was horrified. He couldn't believe that Brahms had offended a man who could have helped both of them. He refused to perform with Brahms anymore.

Franz Liszt playing the piano. When Brahms met him in 1853, Liszt was famous throughout Europe for his virtuoso piano technique and his many compositions.

In some desperation, Brahms returned to Joachim. He stayed for weeks and then months, and his parents became frantic. He wasn't touring, he was burying himself in a small town with no apparent means of making a living. They even offered him Fritz's life savings to help him continue his tour. Fritz must have been furious. Once again his parents were showing him that they thought his older brother was more important than he was.

Joachim sent the Brahmses a reassuring letter filled with extravagant praise for his new friend. "How splendid it will be when his artistic powers are revealed in a work accessible to all! And with his ardent desire for perfection, nothing else is possible," he wrote. These comments made them feel much better.

Eventually the two young men put on a concert, earning Brahms enough money to strike out on a solo walking tour of western Germany. Along the way he made several valuable musical contacts, and nearly all of them echoed Joachim's parting words to him: "You must call on Robert Schumann."

Brahms was reluctant at first. Several years earlier he had sent a packet of his compositions to Schumann. It was returned unopened. He also recalled his unhappy visit with Liszt. But he summoned up his courage. He would call upon the great man.

It was a decision that would transform his life—in more ways than one. ◆

Monitor and *Merrimac*

One of the most momentous events in the history of naval warfare occurred in the U.S. Civil War on March 9, 1862, with what is popularly known as the Battle of the *Monitor* and the *Merrimac*. For centuries before that event, battles had been fought between wooden sailing vessels.

Soon after the outbreak of the Civil War in April 1861, Confederate forces approached the Union naval base at Norfolk, Virginia. Union forces scuttled one of their finest ships, the USS *Merrimac*, a large wooden sailing ship. The Confederates quickly raised it. Rather than restore the ship to its original condition, they decided on a daring scheme: They would cover it with three-inch-thick iron plating. That would protect it from enemy cannon fire.

Because there were many spies during the Civil War, the Union found out what was going on. They frantically began an effort to build a similar armored ship. While both ships were similar under water, their designs above the waterline were totally different. The *Virginia,* as the Confederates had renamed the *Merrimac,* resembled a long, narrow house with sloping walls and a flat roof. There were openings for six big guns.

The *Monitor,* on the other hand, was considerably smaller. The deck was flat and very close to the water. There was a tiny wheelhouse up forward and a revolving turret with two big guns in the center.

On March 8, 1862, the *Virginia* crept from her dock and headed for a nearby fleet of the Union ships. She easily destroyed two before darkness. She returned to port, expecting to sink the remaining ships.

But the *Monitor* had been finished just in time. She arrived late that afternoon, but was too far away to help. It was a different story the following day. The two ships met in a battle. Neither ship could do much damage to the other. Finally the fighting ended in a draw.

The *Virginia* returned to her dock. Several months later, as Union forces closed in on Norfolk, the Confederates blew her up. Eventually *Monitor* tried to steam back north. She encountered a storm, and water began pouring down into the hull. Most of the crew was rescued, but more than a dozen couldn't get off in time. She sank in more than 200 feet of water.

The battle marked a huge change in naval warfare. From then on, navies around the world would build only iron and steel ships. The day of the wooden combat ship was over.

Clara Schumann plays the piano while her husband Robert looks on. Robert Schumann was a famous composer who wrote a very flattering magazine article about Brahms that made the young man instantly famous. But soon after writing it, Schumann was committed to a mental asylum and died there two years later.

Masters of Music

CHAPTER 4

In and Out of Love

The flattering article that Schumann wrote was just the tip of the iceberg of his influence. Both Schumann and his wife, Clara, kept detailed diaries. The entries for the dates of Brahms's visit are filled with praise for the young man. Robert Schumann introduced Brahms to his circle of friends, many of whom were important in the music world. He also recommended him to a large music publishing company. Thanks to Schumann, Johannes Brahms was obscure no longer.

It was a truly joyous Christmas in 1853 for the Brahms family. Hannes had begun to see his compositions in print. He was the talk of Hamburg. People from all over the city dropped in to visit the now famous young man. Meanwhile, Johann Jakob received a promotion.

Two months later Johannes Brahms's life was again in turmoil.

Robert Schumann attempted suicide.

Schumann had been in precarious mental health for much of his life. In recent years his condition had grown worse. He began hearing voices in his head. He even feared that he would do harm to Clara and their children.

In late February he became so desperate that he threw himself into the Rhine River. He was pulled out before he drowned. Then he was committed to a private mental hospital near Bonn.

The conditions there were relatively pleasant. Schumann wasn't locked up, and he was allowed to wander the grounds. He even had a piano in his room.

None of this eased his suffering. Clara wasn't allowed to see him. The doctors were afraid that that would be too disturbing and exciting for him. They did allow some of his friends, particularly Brahms, to visit him. Clara would eagerly await each new report on Robert's condition.

Now thirty-four, Clara was left with six children and another one on the way. She also had bills to pay—but she refused to accept charity. Because she was a gifted pianist, she began touring and giving recitals. This helped financially and must have provided some relief from her constant worries.

Brahms felt a sense of duty to the man who had given him so much. He immediately returned to the Schumann household. He helped the servants take care of the Schumann children and took over managing the family's finances.

Duty soon turned into something else. Brahms fell in love with Clara Schumann. She was a beautiful and highly intelligent woman who thoroughly understood music. And Clara must have felt some attraction to Brahms in return. He was handsome with bright blue eyes that he had inherited from his mother.

But she was fourteen years older than he was—and still married to someone else. Not surprisingly, it was a turbulent period for the young man.

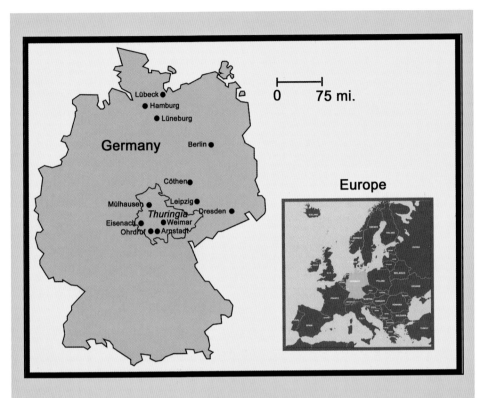

A map of present-day Germany. Johannes Brahms began his life in Hamburg.

In late July, 1856, Robert's doctors realized that his end was near. Clara was finally allowed to visit her husband. It was a touching scene. Robert licked wine from her fingers and they hugged each other.

He died two days later.

Now that she was a widow, Clara could have married Johannes. That never happened. Perhaps they felt that marriage would have betrayed their fond memories of Robert Schumann. They were also aware of the gossip about them. That may have made them reluctant to get more involved with each other. Within a year, they went their separate ways. But they always remained extremely close friends.

Clara even helped Brahms get a position with the Prince of Detmold for a couple of months during the winter each year, giving piano lessons to the ladies of the court and leading a small choir. He also gave piano lessons in Hamburg and founded a women's chorus, which he conducted.

In the summer of 1858 Brahms met Agathe von Siebold. She was twenty-three and had a beautiful singing voice. Soon they exchanged engagement rings.

January 1859 saw the premiere of Brahms's First Piano Concerto. Brahms played the piano part himself. When the final notes sounded, a few people clapped. That faint approval was followed by the sound of many more people hissing. Brahms rose to his feet, shook the conductor's hand, then walked off the stage. It had been a disaster. One critic wrote, "The public was wearied and the musicians puzzled."

It was a disaster in another way. The harsh words that followed the concerto's premiere didn't offer much encouragement that

A photo of the elderly Johannes Brahms and a lady friend. Brahms enjoyed the company of women but he never married.

Brahms would soon be able to support a wife and family with his music.

He sent Agathe a letter. He wrote, "I love you! I must see you again! But I cannot wear fetters [chains]! Write to me, whether I am to come back, to take you in my arms, to kiss you and tell you that I love you."

In essence, he told her that despite his love for her, he could not marry her. Agathe was heartbroken. She wrote him back, breaking off the engagement. The two never saw each other again.

Friends who knew them both were furious. Some refused to speak with him again. Brahms himself wrote, "I've played the scoundrel toward Agathe."

It was probably his best chance of getting married. Though he would have future romances, he would always back away from commitment.

Later that year his spirits rose. His concerto was performed in Hamburg, and this time the reception was more favorable. Meanwhile he was composing many other works. He also believed that he would be appointed as the successor to the retiring conductor of the Philharmonic Concerts in Hamburg. Almost on the spur of the moment, in September 1862 he decided to take an extended trip to Vienna. He viewed this trip as a long vacation before taking over the job.

His first reaction to Vienna was positive. "I have established myself here within ten paces of the Prater and can drink my wine where Beethoven drank his. Since I can't have it any better, I find things quite cheerful and attractive."

When he returned, his hopes for the Hamburg position were dashed. The decision had gone in favor of another man.

Brahms could never have imagined that it was the last time he would live in his native city. ◆

The Olympic Games began in 776 B.C. in the village of Olympia, Greece. After several days of religious festivities, a single sports event was held in a large open field next to the temples. It was a sprint of just under 200 yards. Spectators sat on banks that surrounded the field on three sides. No women were allowed to compete or to watch.

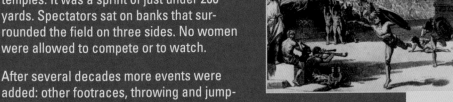

After several decades more events were added: other footraces, throwing and jumping, horse and chariot races, boxing and wrestling. In one brutal event called the pankration, a combination of boxing and wrestling, almost anything was allowed. Sometimes the winner would kill his opponent. In one famous case the winner himself died while his opponent survived.

People traveled from all over Greece to compete in the Olympics. They were held at four-year intervals for more than 1,000 years. But with the rise of Christianity, they were regarded as a shameful pagan ritual and were suppressed.

Late in the nineteenth century, a group of European aristocrats under the leadership of Baron Pierre de Coubertin decided to revive the Olympics. They had studied ancient Greek literature and history as schoolboys. Because the original site at Olympia was in ruins and was too remote, the first modern Olympics were held in Athens, the capital of Greece and its largest city. The year was 1896.

Most of the athletes in that Olympics were from Greece. Only twelve other countries had entries. All were men. All together, about 300 athletes competed in 43 events in nine different sports: track and field, bicycle racing, fencing, gymnastics, shooting, swimming, tennis, weightlifting, and wrestling.

Today, of course, the Olympics—which are still held every four years—are one of the world's biggest and most important sporting events. More than 100 countries send thousands of athletes. There are almost as many competitions for women as there are for men.

A photo of Johannes Brahms as a middle-aged man. It was probably taken soon after he grew the beard that became one of his most distinguishing characteristics for the rest of his life. Compare this illustration with the one on p. 6.

Masters of Music

CHAPTER 5

Fame and the Final Years

Brahms returned to Vienna, where he was offered the position of directing the Vienna Singakademie, a choral group. That helped to make up for his disappointment over losing the Hamburg job. He resigned after two years. By that time, however, his hard work was beginning to pay off in other ways. He was acquiring a reputation as an important composer.

He returned briefly to Hamburg in June 1864 to try to help his parents save their marriage. Most people believe that the age difference finally resulted in stresses that doomed it. Whatever the cause, the marriage ended.

In January 1865 Christiane Brahms died. The shock of losing her spurred Johannes to resume work on his *German Requiem,* which he had begun in 1857. His father remarried in the fall of 1865. This time Johann Jakob went in the other direction, as his new wife was eighteen years younger than he was. She also had a son. By then Johann Jakob had reached the level that at one time he had hoped his son might reach: He was a member of the Hamburg Philharmonic.

Johannes Brahms spent the next few years traveling frequently on short concert tours, either playing the piano or conducting. He also made a number of important and influential friends. Slowly but steadily both his reputation and his standard of living were increasing.

By 1868 he felt confident enough to settle permanently in Vienna. That was also the year that his *German Requiem* premiered. It cemented his reputation.

A very short song he composed that same year is probably more familiar to millions of people than his longer works. It is *Wiegenlied,* or "Cradle Song," more popularly known as "Brahms's Lullaby." It begins with the words "Lullaby, and good night." By the time it ends four verses later, the child to whom it is being sung is often fast asleep.

Four years later, in 1872, his father died of liver cancer. Several months after the funeral, Brahms became conductor of the Vienna Gesellschaftskonzerte.

In 1875 he resigned his position with the Gesellschaftskonzerte. By then he had become famous not just in Germany but all over the world. He would spend the rest of his life doing what he wished, which was to compose and occasionally conduct concerts of his own music. He could live comfortably off the income from his concerts and royalties from his compositions.

These compositions finally included his First Symphony, which he wrote in 1876. That inaugurated one of the most fruitful periods of composition in music history. The Second Symphony appeared in 1877, and was followed by the Violin Concerto (1879), Piano Concerto #2 (1881), Third Symphony (1883), Fourth Symphony (1885), and the Concerto for Violin and Cello (1887).

Honors were pouring in. In the mid-1870s England's prestigious Cambridge University offered him an honorary doctorate in music, though he declined to accept it because he didn't want to make the lengthy trip. In 1878 his native Hamburg performed a concert of his music. It must have been especially satisfying to return to the city where he had played the piano in waterfront taverns thirty years before and be recognized for the quality of his music.

The following year the University of Breslau awarded him an honorary doctorate. He wrote a brief note to the University, thanking them for recognizing his accomplishments. Then his friend Joachim told him that the school expected something a little more substantial—a musical composition. So he wrote the *Academic Festival Overture*.

In 1887 the German emperor, Kaiser Wilhelm, gave Brahms one of Germany's most prestigious awards, the Pour le Mérite ("for merit") of the Order of Peace. Sixteen years earlier Brahms had dedicated his *Triumphlied* ("Song of Triumph") to the Kaiser after a German victory in the Franco-Prussian War.

His life settled into a comfortable pattern. He would give concerts in the winter and compose during the summer. He often took trips during those warmer months, but he was still disciplined enough to work on his music.

He became a familiar figure on Vienna's streets and in the best houses. The man who had been slim and clean-shaven when he was young was now very heavy after years of eating the rich food of his adopted city. He sported a long, bushy beard.

As the 1890s dawned, things began to change. Brahms went through all his old compositions, destroying many of them. Several of his close friends died. So did his sister and brother.

The worst shock came on May 20, 1896, with the death of his beloved Clara Schumann. He caught a chill at her funeral. Soon afterward he complained of not feeling well. He went to see a doctor, who discovered that his patient suffered from liver cancer—the same disease that had killed his father.

He went into a gradual decline, making his final public appearance on March 7 the following year. The highlight was a performance of his Fourth Symphony. Applause came after each movement, and there was a thunderous ovation when the final note sounded. Everyone watched the now frail figure rise unsteadily to his feet.

Johannes Brahms died on April 3, 1897.

A friend wrote to Joachim a few days later, "I was at the funeral of our beloved Brahms in Vienna. I had to witness the unbelievable with my own eyes. The extent of our loss cannot be measured."

Johannes Brahms and the great Russian composer Peter Ilyich Tchaikovsky lived at almost the same time. But it is hard to imagine two more different personalities. Tchaikovsky wore his heart on his sleeve. He wrote long letters in which he poured out his inner feelings.

Brahms would never have done anything like that. He kept his emotions carefully in check.

One friend said, "His deepest feelings were his own and no one else's. Anything which smacked of sentiment he abhorred and said so."

Even Clara Schumann, who probably knew him better than anyone else, wrote, "To me he is as much a riddle—I might almost say as much a stranger—as he was 25 years ago."

He maintained a gruff exterior that seemed almost designed to keep people at arm's length. "I am a difficult person to get along with," he wrote. One time he left a party, saying, "If there is anybody here I have not insulted, I apologize."

Yet after he became successful, he was generous with his money. He provided financial support for his father's widow and her son. He helped many younger artists, both composers and performers, get started.

One of them was the granddaughter of the man who had taken him in during the summers of 1847 and 1848. She needed a recommendation for a music scholarship. Brahms not only supplied the

An illustration of the interior of Johannes Brahms's house in Vienna. He moved there in 1871 and it remained his residence until his death 26 years later.

recommendation but also offered to pay for the scholarship himself if there wasn't enough money.

"I am indebted to the family of the girl for much love and friendship, and my memory of her grandfather is one of the most beautiful kind that the human heart can treasure," he wrote.

Brahms always remained grateful to Marxsen, his composition teacher. He maintained a regular correspondence with him, dedicated his Second Piano Concerto to him, and paid for the printing of one of Marxsen's favorite compositions during celebrations honoring his "fiftieth anniversary as an artist" in 1883.

Marxsen, then seventy-seven, was touched by the gesture. He wrote, "What a surprise, what a great pleasure you have given me! In my old age it has been granted to me to see a second day of triumph in my artistic career."

Then he added that Brahms was "the pride of my life and professional career. I want to clasp you to my heart, the loyal friend, who had employed his heavenly gifts for the true welfare of Art."

Millions of concert-goers would agree. In the years following his death, Brahms would share yet another quality with his musical idol, Beethoven. The symphonies and concertos composed by Johannes Brahms and Ludwig van Beethoven are more popular in the world's concert halls than those of any other composers.

FRANCO-PRUSSIAN WAR

When Brahms was born, Germany as we know it today didn't exist. Rather, the territory was occupied by several hundred kingdoms and provinces of various sizes.

Among this group, one of the largest and most important was Prussia. Its chancellor, Otto von Bismarck, dreamed of uniting all these states into a single powerful nation. Prussia would provide the leadership.

After Napoleon's defeat at Waterloo in 1815, Europe existed without any major wars for half a century. In 1866, when Prussia defeated Austria in the Seven Weeks' War, France became uneasy. French leaders worried that Prussia was becoming too powerful.

Bismarck encouraged them to worry. He believed that a war with France would bring about the unification of Germany. He made sure that Russia, Italy, and Great Britain wouldn't become involved. Both sides began preparing for war.

The spark that ignited the flames came when Spain needed a new king following a revolution. The leader of the rebel forces offered the throne to a Prussian prince. On Bismarck's advice, Prussia accepted.

The French protested. The last thing they wanted was a strong German influence on their southern border. Under pressure from the French, the Prussians reversed their decision and declined the offer. However, when the French made further demands and Prussia refused, France declared war. It was July 19, 1870.

The French quickly discovered that the Prussians had been much better at their preparations for war. Prussian armies—which also included men from many of the other German kingdoms—defeated the French in battle after battle. Within three months they reached Paris and began a siege. The desperate citizens had to eat dogs, cats, and even rats to survive.

The French surrendered early in 1871. They had to pay Germany one billion dollars and give up the German-speaking provinces of Alsace and Lorraine, which they had previously brought under their control.

Bismarck had achieved his goal. The German Empire was created under the leadership of Kaiser Wilhelm I of Prussia.

Selected Works

Symphonies
Symphony #1
Symphony #2
Symphony #3
Symphony #4

Concertos
Piano Concerto #1
Piano Concerto #2
Violin Concerto
Double Concerto for Violin and Cello

Other Orchestral Works
Variations on a Theme by Haydn
Academic Festival Overture
Tragic Overture

Choral Works
A German Requiem
Alto Rhapsody for Alto, Male Chorus
    and Orchestra
Schicksalslied—Song of Destiny for
    Chorus and Orchestra

Piano Works
Hungarian Dances
Liebeslieder Waltzes for Piano Four
    Hands
Variations for Piano Four Hands on a
    Theme by Schumann
Variations and Fugue for Piano on a
    Theme by Handel

Chronology

1833 Born on May 7 in Hamburg, Germany
1837 Starts taking music lessons from father
1839 Begins attending school
1840 Begins piano lessons with Friedrich Cossel
1843 Makes first public appearance as pianist; begins lessons with Eduard Marxsen
1846 Begins playing for money in Hamburg taverns
1848 Gives first solo concert
1853 Meets Robert and Clara Schumann
1858 Meets Agathe von Siebold and becomes engaged, but later breaks it off
1859 Premiere of First Piano Concerto
1862 Visits Vienna for first time
1863 Becomes conductor of Vienna Singakademie
1865 Mother dies
1868 Settles permanently in Vienna; *German Requiem* premieres
1872 Father dies; accepts position as conductor of the Vienna Gesellschaftskonzerte
1875 Resigns as conductor of the Vienna Gesellschaftskonzerte
1876 Premiere of First Symphony
1878 Travels to Hamburg for concert of his works
1879 Awarded honorary doctorate by Breslau University
1885 Premiere of Fourth Symphony
1896 Clara Schumann dies
1897 Dies on April 3

1827 Ludwig van Beethoven dies

1836 Siege of the Alamo in Texas

1837 Queen Victoria of England begins sixty-four-year reign

1840 Russian composer Peter Tchaikovsky is born

1841 Belgian instrument maker Adolphe Sax invents the saxophone

1846 U.S.-Mexico war begins; ends two years later as Arizona, California, Nevada, New Mexico, Texas, Utah, and parts of Colorado and Wyoming are added to United States

1853 In New York, Henry Steinway and his three sons open what becomes one of the most famous piano manufacturing companies

1854 Crimean War begins

1857 U.S. engineer E. G. Otis installs first safety elevator

1859 Charles Darwin publishes *Origin of Species;* work on Suez Canal begins

1861 U.S. Civil War begins

1862 Battle of *Monitor* and *Merrimac* changes naval warfare forever

1865 Abraham Lincoln assassinated; Civil War ends

1866 Alfred Nobel invents dynamite

1868 First professional baseball team, Cincinnati Red Stockings, is formed

1869 Princeton and Rutgers play first formal intercollegiate football game

1875 Premiere of French composer Georges Bizet's *Carmen*, one of the world's most famous operas

1876 First complete performance of German composer Richard Wagner's *Ring des Nibelungen*, which consists of four separate operas and lasts for a total of nearly twenty hours

1877 Thomas Edison patents the phonograph

1878 Thomas Edison patents the electric lightbulb

1883 New York's Metropolitan Opera opens

1888 Composer Irving Berlin is born

1889 Adolf Hitler is born

1893 Henry Ford builds his first automobile; Peter Tchaikovsky dies

1895 Wilhelm Roentgen discovers X rays

1896 The Olympic Games are revived

1902 Italian tenor Enrico Caruso makes his first phonograph recording

1904 First radio transmission of music occurs in Graz, Austria

1905 Albert Einstein proposes his special theory of relativity

Further Reading

For Young Adults

Brown, Jonathan. *Johannes Brahms: An Essential Guide to His Life and Works.* London: Pavilion Books Limited, 1996.

Holmes, Paul. *Brahms (Illustrated Lives of the Great Composers).* London: Omnibus Press, 1992.

Video recording. *A Look at the Life and Times of Johannes Brahms.* West Long Branch, N.J.: Kultur International Films, 1996.

Works Consulted

Styra Avins with Josef Eisinger, ed. *Johannes Brahms: Life and Letters.* Oxford University Press, 1997.

Becker, Heinz. "Brahms," in *The New Grove Late Romantic Masters.* Stanley Sadie, ed. New York: W.W. Norton, 1985.

Botstein, Leon. *The Compleat Brahms.* New York: W.W. Norton & Company, 1999.

Burnett, James. *Brahms: A Critical Study.* New York: Praeger, 1972.

Gal, Hans. Translated by Joseph Stein. *Johannes Brahms: His Work and Personality.* Westport, Conn.: Greenwood Press, 1963.

Geiringer, Karl. *Brahms: His Life and Work.* New York: Da Capo Press, 1982.

MacDonald, Malcolm. *Brahms.* New York: Schirmer Books, 1990.

Schonberg, Harold C. *The Lives of the Great Composers.* Third edition. New York: W.W. Norton, 1997.

Swafford, Jan. *Johannes Brahms: A Biography.* New York: Alfred A. Knopf, 1998.

Internet Addresses

http://www.aroundgreece.com/olympics-modern.html

http://www.classicalarchives.com/brahms.html

http://www.johannesbrahms.org

http://www.nobel.se/nobel/alfred-nobel/biographical/index.html

http://www.mariner.org

http://music.mpr.org/features/9607_schumann/cschumann3.htm

Glossary

abhor (ab-HOR)—To dislike intensely.

adulation (ad-joo-LAY-shun)—A high degree of praise.

concerto (kon-CHAIR-toe)—A musical composition for orchestra and solo instrument, usually written in three movements.

idyllic (eye-DILL-ick)—In a peaceful and natural setting.

pagan (PAY-gun)—A person or group believing in more than one god.

recital (ree-SITE-al)—A public musical performance, usually by one person.

requiem (REH-kwee-um)—A Catholic mass, or religious ceremony, for the dead.

symphony (SIM-foe-nee)—A large-scale musical composition for full orchestra, usually consisting of four movements.

tutelage (TOO-tuh-lij)—The guidance or instruction of a teacher.

virtuoso (ver-choo-OH-so)—A musician with exceptional talent.

Index